FINDING
AGENT
RIGHT

FINDING AGENT RIGHT

For Your Best Real Estate Deal

Ask the right questions and get the right answers before choosing your real estate agent.

LARRY STOLLER

To order additional copies of this book, contact:
Xlibris Corporation
1-888-795-4274
www.Xlibris.com
Orders@Xlibris.com
37650

Contents

For Flora, Harry, Helene, and Heather

Find the Right Real Estate Agent
to Work for You

Honest, competent, innovative, communicative, and personable—these are the most desirable traits to look for when choosing your real estate agent. Committed to representing you exclusively and getting you the best real estate deal—these should be your agent's top priorities.

In *Finding Agent Right,* Larry Stoller mixes knowledge with humor in a simple format that makes it easy to find an agent with those characteristics and commitments. By asking the right questions and getting the right answers, you will be better prepared to choose the agent who will work best for you.

Filled with reassuring insights, *Finding Agent Right* is like a trustworthy friend at your side as you make important real estate decisions.

Don't be content to settle for anything less than *Agent Right!*

Why This Book?

So why did I write this book?

Well, it has to do with that classic television commercial about Charlie, the tuna. I can remember Charlie doing everything that he could to show that he had good taste. I used to feel bad for poor old Charlie. No matter what he did, StarKist (the tuna distributing company) would always come back with the same response: "Sorry, Charlie. StarKist wants tuna that tastes good, not tuna with good taste."

That's why I wrote this book. I don't want you to wind up with some unscrupulous Charlie who looks good but leaves a bad taste in your mouth. These characters give the real estate industry a bad name. So I have devised an easy way to weed them out.

A bad agent inevitably drops the ball or passes it on to someone else. Problems come up that could have been prevented or should have been resolved but were not. Either the agent didn't pick up on these problems or was not even there to deal with them. And the longer problems are left unresolved, the more difficult they become to fix.

If you're selling or buying real estate, make sure you get the right agent. How do you do that? Use this guide to hire Agent Right!

Common problems include the following:

- purchase agreement errors
- missing addendums
- missing amendments
- incorrect use of forms

- unsatisfied contingencies
- incomplete house repairs
- liens on the house
- missing insurance binders
- delayed appraisals
- additional underwriting conditions
- incomplete funding package
- closing statement mistakes

Can these problems threaten or break a deal? Yes. Can all of them be avoided? Absolutely!

Bad agents see these problems all the time. Good agents see them less frequently. That's because good agents prepare and submit correct and complete documentation. They also follow up and communicate with all parties of the transaction. It's this attention to detail and oversight that prevent good transactions from going bad!

Agents need to be directly involved in the transaction every step of the way until it is closed. That's when the deal is done, the seller gets the money, the buyer gets the house, and the agents get paid.

So when choosing a real estate agent, make sure that your agent will be *working for you* throughout the entire transaction. You deserve a good agent, a good transaction, and a great real estate experience. I don't think you should settle for anything less.

Good-bye, Charlie. Hello, Agent Right!

Realty's Believe It or Not

**Like *Ripley's Believe It or Not*,
Here's Realty's Believe It or Not**

On the Market for Just Two Weeks

SELLER: My home's been listed for two weeks now and there's only been one showing. What's the problem?

AGENT: The market is really bad now. We'd better lower the price. Right now, it's at $499,900. Let's get it below four to $399,900.

First Time out with the Buyer

BUYER: I really love this house. How much should I offer?

AGENT: It's the perfect house for you. You may want to come in with a full price offer or maybe more than what they're asking.

One Day before the Closing

SELLERS: Do we need to bring anything to the closing tomorrow?

AGENT: No, you don't. But it's a good thing that you called. It looks like the closing may be delayed a day. Something about the loan package and final approval for the buyer.

At the Closing: Seller's Net Proceeds

SELLERS: You said we'd net about $141,000. This statement says cash to seller is $91,000.

AGENT: I'm pretty sure I gave you a net proceeds estimate sheet. I don't see one in the paperwork that I have. Do you have yours with you? We can compare the figures.

After the Closing: The New House

BUYERS: We're moving into our new home, but the window shades have been removed, there are no appliances in the kitchen, the washer and dryer are gone, and the walls and doors are all banged up.

AGENT: I don't understand. We did our walk-through last week and everything was okay.

Folks, can you believe what you've just read?

I can tell you that buyers and sellers hear these things from their agents time and time again. That's because they had the wrong agents, the agents who didn't do their jobs right.

These mishaps and mistakes should never happen.
But unfortunately, they do, and the chances of them happening to you will increase if you hire the wrong agent.

Here's how you can make sure you hire the right agent to work for you:

- Interview at least three agents before making a decision.
- Ask them the questions in this book that are most important to you.
- Compare their answers against one another and against Agent Right's answers.
- Determine if the agents will put what they say they will do in writing.
- Choose the agent with the best answers to be your Agent Right.

Selling a Home

Selling a home is one of the largest financial transactions you'll make in your lifetime. With variable commission rates, complex transactions, changing market conditions, and many real estate companies to choose from, you need to hire the right agent and get the best deal.

For sellers, that means

- the house is optimally priced and effectively marketed;
- the offers and counteroffers are successfully negotiated;
- the contract is complete and correct;
- the closing goes smoothly; and
- you, the seller, realize the greatest net proceeds possible.

Here are the questions and answers that relate to selling a home:

SELLER: So how much do you think my home will sell for?

AGENT: Based upon this CMA (comparative market analysis), your home should sell somewhere between $400,000 and $500,000.

AGENT RIGHT: Folks, that's too big a spread. If an agent truly knows his or her market, a $25,000 price range (for a home priced somewhere between $400,000 and $500,000) would be acceptable. A good rule of thumb would be that the price range should not exceed 5 percent of the highest suggested selling price. Pricing a home correctly is critical. When a property is first listed, it generates a very high level of interest from many prospective buyers. That level of interest declines dramatically over time. Therefore, your price needs to be in line.

NOTE: Don't just take the agent with the highest price. He or she could just be looking for a listing agreement.

SELLER: Should I hold out for the highest price?

AGENT: If I were you, I would accept any price that falls within that price range in the CMA.

AGENT RIGHT: That's not a sound strategy. If the offer is high up in the price range, then it might be a good idea to accept it. But even then, it would still depend on what the rest of the terms were. For example, are you being asked to pay any closing or loan-related costs? Are you being asked for a decorating allowance? Does the closing date and possession date work for you? It's also important to know the market. If it's a seller's market, then holding out for the highest price makes sense. Whereas in a buyer's market, any offer in the price range would be acceptable.

SELLER: What exactly is a CMA?

AGENT: It's a determination of the current market value of your home.

AGENT RIGHT: It's much more than that. The CMA (comparative market analysis) is a comprehensive analysis to determine the correct selling price and the best marketing strategy for your home. The correct selling price is the highest possible price the market will bear. While some agents seem to pull this number out of the air, others may subject you to a fifty-page thesis. So which one do you believe?

For starters, have at least three CMA presentations. There's no charge, no obligation, and they should be interesting and informative. It's a good idea to let the respective agents know that you will be interviewing three of them. That should prevent them from pressuring you too much. It will also motivate them to produce an outstanding analysis for you, maybe even give you their best deal.

During the presentation and interview, keep an eye out for the following things:

- Look for comparable homes that are currently for sale to compare your home against the competition.
- Look for comparable homes that were recently sold or pended (sold but not yet closed) to obtain a clear picture of how the market has valued homes that are comparable to yours. These are the same sales statistics that banks and other lending institutions analyze to determine how much they can lend to qualified buyers.
- Look for comparable homes that failed to sell (i.e., cancelled or expired) to avoid pricing at a level that would not attract buyers.
- Look for a marketing plan that clearly spells out the methods that will be used to promote your property to the widest possible audience of prospective buyers.

Finally, make the agent stand behind his or her market analysis and price determination. Ask for a way out of the listing agreement if there is no progress made in selling your home. It would be best to ask for this at the end of the CMA sales presentation. It could be jotted down on the last page of the presentation. It should say that if the agent does not act in accordance with the methods and objectives in the marketing plan and/or the plan is not working (not resulting in showings, feedback, or offers) after forty-five days, the seller may

- ask the agent for a revision of the plan, or
- cancel the listing agreement.

SELLER: How long should it take for my home to sell?

AGENT: Somewhere between three and six months.

AGENT RIGHT: If an agent is good at analyzing the available home selling statistics and understands the current market conditions, "within a specific number of months" would be a better response. The time it takes to sell your home will be affected by the price and the condition of the home. With the right marketing, your home could sell in less than a week.

SELLER: What if my house doesn't sell within that time frame?

AGENT: We'll lower the price and extend the listing.

AGENT RIGHT: Here's what your response should be to that agent: "Okay, I'll lower my price if you'll lower your commission." An agent should stand behind the pricing of your home. If the house was priced right in the first place and then effectively marketed, it should have sold. Valuable market time would not have been lost. Sometimes an unscrupulous agent may suggest a higher price to get the listing. Then when it doesn't sell, the agent tells you the price is too high. Before you sign a listing agreement, ask the agent if he or she believes that your home will sell in the suggested price range. If the agent says yes, then ask that agent to agree to lower the commission if the house does not sell in the price range suggested. What can be fairer than that? If the agent won't agree to that, don't list with him or her.

SELLER: How much commission do you charge?

AGENT: Our company charges 7 percent. That's for full service and proven results.

AGENT RIGHT: That may be a true statement, but how much service do you actually need and how much money do you want to pay? It's a good idea to shop around for agents and companies, not just for price, but for services offered and proven results. A good way to accomplish this is by speaking to real estate company broker-managers by telephone or by reviewing their company Web sites.

SELLER: How are commission rates determined?

AGENT: This is the rate that the firms around here charge.

AGENT RIGHT: That's the wrong answer and the wrong agent. There's no set rate in any area. That would imply price-fixing, a big no-no in the real estate industry. Fees and commissions are independently established and usually based upon the quality and quantity of services provided. When discussing rates, there are two rates of commission that you should be aware of:

- the total rate of commission that you, the seller will be required to pay, and
- included in that total commission, the rate of commission that will be paid out to the company bringing in the buyer.

For example, one company may charge a total of 6 percent and pay out 3 percent. Another company may charge 7 percent and pay out 3.5 percent.

SELLER: I've heard of discount real estate companies. Should I talk to them?

AGENT: I'd be careful about those discount companies as nobody will show their listings.

AGENT RIGHT: That's not true. Real estate is very competitive, and there are a variety of business models out there, giving the consumer many choices. It's a good idea to talk to different companies and compare their commissions and their services to find the one that's best for you. You may be pleasantly surprised to find that your home will be shown just as much and maybe more regardless of the amount of commission that you pay.

SELLER: I want to pay less commission. What can you do for me?

AGENT: If you go with us, I'll see if the manager will agree to 6 percent instead of 7 percent. And you'll still get all of our services.

AGENT RIGHT: The manager will, and I'll bet the agent already knows that. But maybe you can do even better! Negotiation is the key here, and if one company won't negotiate, another company will. Do you really need all of their services, or can you get by with a little less? If you can get by with less, then you should pay less commission. You know, some companies may give you more services and still charge you less commission. It's best to compare and negotiate.

SELLER: Do you have any other options that would work better for me?

AGENT: No, but I can get the job done to your full satisfaction for 6 percent. Will that work?

AGENT RIGHT: There are many options available to the savvy seller. They include the following: for sale by owner, for sale by owner with assistance, online listing service, limited MLS (multiple listing service), full MLS, discount real estate companies with limited service, discount real estate companies with full service, local full-service companies, and national full-service companies. For example, in the "for sale by owner" option, you might be doing everything on your own. With the "online listing service," you should receive ongoing exposure to many prospective buyers. If you went with a full-service company, many agents would be trying to sell your home. Choose the option and company that works best for you.

SELLER: Does being in a "seller's market" or a "buyer's market" affect the commission that I pay?

AGENT: Not really. For the 7 percent, you'll get our full service regardless of what the market is.

AGENT RIGHT: That may be that company's policy, but current market conditions will have an effect on how homes are sold and marketed. Therefore, some companies might consider modifying the commissions accordingly. For example, in a seller's market, the broker's job is much easier. There's less work to do, fewer resources to be expended, and the sale cycle is considerably shorter. This might be a very good time to negotiate a lower commission. On the other hand, in a buyer's market, maybe that 7 percent is a good deal all around (depending upon what and how much the agent and real estate company will do for you).

SELLER: If it's a buyer's market, do I have to pay additional commission?

AGENT: No, you'll still pay 7 percent.

AGENT RIGHT: You won't have to pay additional commission per se, but it will probably cost you more to sell your home. That's because in a buyer's market, the brokerage may have to offer incentives to buyers and cash bonuses to selling agents to make their listings more competitive. And the seller usually winds up paying for these.

SELLER: How can I make my home more attractive to the buyer in a "buyer's market"?

AGENT: By keeping your home spotless, picture-perfect, and always ready to show.

AGENT RIGHT: Great advice. You want to wow them as they drive up the driveway and as they enter the house. However, in a real buyer's market, you and your real estate agent may have to do even more. You may have to offer a home warranty on all mechanicals and appliances or a decorating allowance or a rebate for closing costs or maybe even a cash bonus to whomever brings in the best offer.

SELLER: Can I cancel the listing before the expiration of the listing contract if my home doesn't sell or if I am not satisfied with your service?

AGENT: No, you have to wait until the listing agreement ends in six months. But if you want something done differently, just let us know.

AGENT RIGHT: This answer is unacceptable. Tell the agent that a cancellation clause has to be included. Make it become effective forty-five days after the date the home was listed. That will give you the option to get out of the listing agreement if your home doesn't sell or if you're not satisfied with the service. The cancellation clause must be written within the listing agreement.

Incidentally, if you are told that your home will sell within three months, then make the listing agreement for three months. If you're told that it will take more than three months to sell, still make the contract for three months and include an option to extend if you so desire. If you decide to extend the listing, you would usually make that decision a few days before the listing expires. At that time, you would meet with the listing agent and modify the listing agreement accordingly. Always state the new expiration date to avoid any confusion. If all terms of the listing agreement remain the same, include a statement to that effect. However, if you and your agent agree to change some of the terms (and it's okay to renegotiate terms and make changes), make sure that those changes are included in the modified listing agreement. You both should sign and date the modified agreement, and that's it. In the absence of a written agreement to extend the listing, the listing agreement expires at midnight on the last day. There's nothing you have to do. You're free to go with another company, sell on your own, or take a breather while you decide what you want to do.

SELLER: I've given some thought to selling on my own or going with a discount company.

AGENT: We'll you can try it; but there are a lot of pitfalls and potential problems, and you won't get the full service and assurances that you'll get from our company.

AGENT RIGHT: If you want to try it on your own, there are plenty of resources and companies that provide advice and assistance. There are books that prepare you for selling on your own. There are for sale by owner shops that will provide you with supplies and forms. There are companies that will offer you online listing services. There are also full-service companies who will partner with you and market your home at the same time that you are trying to sell your home on your own.

SELLER: Everything you said sounds very positive. Can we modify the listing agreement to include some of what you have said?

AGENT: Oh, we can't do that. The listing agreement is standard and specific as it is. But we can certainly modify our marketing plans to include all of your concerns.

AGENT RIGHT: (I don't believe I'm hearing this.) The listing agreement is the contract that spells out the specific terms that the seller and real estate brokerage agree to. And like any contract, it can be modified to include what is agreed upon. If it's written in the listing agreement, then that's the way it is. If it's not written in the agreement, then it will not happen.

I'm going to repeat something now that I said before. The seller should add a cancellation clause that allows termination of the listing agreement before the expiration date. Now we have to be reasonable here; we are not trying to hang the agent. We just want a way out if we are dissatisfied with the service we're getting.

Buying a Home

Buying a home is one of the largest financial commitments you will make in your lifetime. With construction costs increasing, home prices rising, market conditions changing, interest rates fluctuating, and numerous funding options to choose from, it's critical that you have the right real estate agent working for you during the entire purchase transaction.

For buyers, that means

- a search for the right house includes the greatest number of houses that are available that meet your requirements;
- the agent or broker can work with your schedule, including evenings and weekends if necessary;
- offers and counteroffers are successfully negotiated;
- a contract is completed correctly;
- your closing is problem-free; and
- you get the best house, the best value, and the best terms for your money

Here are the questions and answers that relate to buying a home:

BUYER: I think I am ready to buy a home, but can I really afford to buy at this time?

AGENT: Your mortgage will not be too much more than your rent. So if you can afford to rent, then you can afford to buy.

AGENT RIGHT: Okay, imagine that you are at home, and it's the weekend. Your air-conditioning stops running, you live in South Carolina, and it's August! Or your heating goes out, you live in Minnesota, and it's January! You're the owner. There's no landlord to fix it. Do you get the picture? Because you will certainly get the bill!

There may be more expenses related to owning a home than renting a home. These expenses may include emergency repairs, routine upkeep, property taxes, utilities, hazard insurance, flood insurance, association fees, lawn care, landscaping, snow removal, and pest control. And do not forget about that one-time down payment.

That being said, I still believe that buying a home is one of the best decisions and investments you can make. I purchased my first home when I was twenty-nine years old. Looking back, I should have bought it earlier. There are tax advantages when you own a home. They may offset some of the additional costs of owning a home. You can also build equity as you pay off your mortgage and the home appreciates in value. It's almost like having a large savings account that gets bigger each year.

The bottom line is that it's important that you prepare an affordability analysis to assess your financial condition. Look at the increase in living costs and see if you can afford a home. When you get prequalified for a home loan, you will get a good idea if you can afford to buy a home and how much home you can afford to buy. You will also receive a good faith estimate of what your closing costs will be. But be careful. The loan officer gets a bigger commission for a bigger loan.

Here are some guidelines that lenders use when determining home affordability for prospective buyers:

- The ratio of your monthly payment to your monthly income should not exceed 28 percent.

- The ratio of your monthly payment plus monthly nonhousing debt to your monthly income should not exceed 36 percent.

NOTE: However, since these rules of thumb are not completely accurate, lenders are not rigid in using them. But you can use them as a simple test of home affordability.

BUYER: How much money will I need to buy a house?

AGENT: Altogether, probably about 10 percent of the cost of the home.

AGENT RIGHT: It will probably be more than 10 percent. When getting a mortgage, the down payment will vary based upon whether it is a primary residence, a second home, a vacation home, or an investment property. Here are some costs to consider: down payment of 10 percent of selling price (usually more but sometimes less), closing costs of 5 percent of selling price, earnest money of 1 percent of selling price (or possibly more), additional escrow, and reserve costs. Sometimes the sellers will pay for all or part of the buyer's closing costs. In any event, it's important to consider cash needed up front and monthly cash outlays as well. That will give you a true picture of how much you will need to buy and to maintain a home.

BUYER: Can I use any of my IRA funds or 401(k) funds for my down payment?

AGENT: Yes, I think you can.

AGENT RIGHT: That's right. You can. The 1997 Taxpayer Relief Act allows first-time home buyers to use up to $10,000 from their IRA with no penalty for a down payment to purchase a home. For the specific rules, check with your accountant or financial advisor or check out http://www.irs.gov/ for IRA rules. You can also take out a loan against your 401(k) company plan. You don't have to be a first-time home buyer to do that. If you take out a loan against your 401(k), it may have to be paid back if you leave your job. Check with your employer for 401(k) loan conditions.

BUYER: You are the listing agent. Is there any advantage for me to work with you?

AGENT: I listed the home, so if you buy it from me, I can get you the best price and the best deal.

AGENT RIGHT: Now, how can that be when the listing agent is trying to get the highest price for the seller? I'd like to know what that agent's plan is for getting you the best price and the best deal. You would want to know also. If you decide to work with the listing agent, remind yourself that the listing agent is representing the seller. Therefore, you'll have to be a good negotiator to get the best deal. Remember, when the listing agent brings in the buyer, he or she gets the full commission. There is no commission to pay to another broker. You could ask the listing agent for a cash rebate at closing. Or maybe you could ask the listing agent for some assistance with paying your closing costs. If the listing agent is not receptive to either of those suggestions, it might be better to hire a different agent to represent you.

BUYER: I am ready to buy a home. How can you help me find the right home?

AGENT: I am a buyer's agent, and I only work with buyers. I will work with you and for you until we find the right home.

AGENT RIGHT: Sounds good and makes sense, but what will that agent do for you that other agents may not do? You will find that different agents have different plans for helping buyers find the home that's right for them. Some agents rely solely on the multiple listing service. Others may include foreclosures and homes that are for sale by owners. And then there are those agents who know how to find homes that are not even on the market. That's right! They can find your dream home before that home is even available for sale. For example, if you know that you want to live in a certain area or a specific development, it's not unusual for an agent to canvass that area with your exact requirements in mind. (As a matter of fact, that's how my wife and I found our dream home in the Hilton Head Island area.)

BUYER: We work during the week. Will you be available to show us homes in the evenings and on weekends?

AGENT: That will not be a problem. I'm part of a team, so if I'm not available, someone else will be.

AGENT RIGHT: Generally, a team is good. But a team can also be bad. For example, aside from you, the person most likely to know what kind of house you want to buy is your agent, not a team.

Sometimes, when more people are involved, there can be more problems and confusion. When you are buying a house, you want your agent with you all the way. That includes evenings and weekends.

BUYER: I'm ready to start looking at homes. What's the next step?

AGENT: First, we'll sign this exclusive buyer's agreement. Then we will determine your exact requirements, get you prequalified, and start looking at homes until you find exactly what you require.

AGENT RIGHT: That sounds reasonable, but it is best to fully understand what this "exclusive buyer's agreement" is all about before signing it. You will also want to be preapproved instead of prequalified. Most sellers will only accept offers from preapproved buyers.

BUYER: What is an "exclusive buyer's agreement"?

AGENT: It is an agreement that states that you agree to work with me exclusively in finding and buying a home. It also explains what our obligations are during the term of the agreement and what fees our company will receive upon the successful closing of the purchase transaction.

AGENT RIGHT: True enough as stated, but it is much more than that! It is the contract between the buyer and the real estate company that includes all the conditions and commitments negotiated and agreed upon. It is also an excellent opportunity for the buyers to put in writing exactly what they expect the agent to do and what the buyers plan to do in conjunction with the agent in finding and purchasing the "right home." In the exclusive buyer's agreement, the buyer should ensure that he or she considers the following factors before signing:

- Is the agent a buyer's broker who is representing only you?
- Are for sale by owner homes included in the agreement? What length of time are you committed to work with the agent?
- How are deals facilitated if you decide on a property that is listed with that same agency?
- Who pays for the agent's services?
- Will your agent's remuneration come solely from the commission that the seller is paying or will you have to pay your agent on an hourly basis or a set fee negotiated in advance?

If you sign an exclusive buyer's agreement, make it for no more than two months, and do not pay anything up front. Two more things to consider:

1) It's okay to modify the exclusive buyer's agreement by adding amendments.
2) Never sign anything that you are not sure about or comfortable signing. Add conditions if you feel they are warranted. If you are going to do a lot of the leg work in researching the listings, locating the homes, eliminating the ones you do not want to see, and only then using your agent to look at the homes you want to see, maybe you should ask for a cash rebate or some other buyer incentive, like a home warranty, inspection credit, or move-in allowance. It has been done many times before.

BUYER: When is the best time of the year to shop for a home?

AGENT: As soon as you are ready to buy before the prices go up.

AGENT RIGHT: The best time depends on your needs, wants, and your resources. Some people can buy anytime; the money's there, and it's not a big issue. But most of us need to get the most for our money. That means buying when more homes are available and when sellers may be willing to lower their prices to compete in a very competitive market. When the housing market begins to slow down, sellers may also be willing to assist you with closing costs. You can usually get a great deal when it's a buyer's market.

BUYER: Do I need a real estate agent to buy a home?

AGENT: You could buy on your own; but without an agent, you will not be represented, and you will not have the assurance that you are getting a good house and a good deal.

AGENT RIGHT: You don't need an agent to buy a home, but a "good agent" will be able to get you a better house, a better value, a better deal, and coordinate all aspects of the transaction. You do not pay for that service either; the seller does. Sometimes agents will offer valuable rebates if you buy through them.

BUYER: How do I know that you are the right real estate agent for me?

AGENT: Here's a list of people I've worked for. They will vouch for me.

AGENT RIGHT: References are good but not good enough. You know what kind of home you are looking for and what kind of lifestyle you want. So you have to find a good agent who understands your needs and wants. That might be a challenge since there are so many agents out there. Here's an approach that I'm sure will work. Call one of the local real estate companies and ask the manager for a referral. Ask your friends or relatives for a referral. After you have some referrals, call them and tell them what you are looking for. Ask them to send you a list and description of the available homes that match your criteria. Then, carefully review what you have received. Were you impressed with the information that they sent you?

If you were, then include that agent in your list of three agents to interview. That approach should improve the quality of the pool of agents that you interview. Take your time with the interview process when looking for Agent Right. Ask the right questions, get the right answers, and choose the agent who will work best for you!

BUYER: Why should I go with your company?

AGENT: We've been around here longer than the others. We know the market better and have more agents and resources to assist you with buying.

AGENT RIGHT: Don't get hung up on how long they've been in business and the number of agents and resources that they have. Focus on the real strength of the company: how resourceful they are, how successful their agents have been, and what the company and agent can do for you today. Look at things like the number of homes they sell, their professionalism, the number of referrals and leads they generate, their knowledge, training, experience, marketing, community involvement, their networking, and the competitive advantages that they have to offer. Remember, the quality of the service that you will receive will depend upon both the company and the agent that you choose.

BUYER: What does dual agency mean, and will it affect me as a buyer?

AGENT: It means that I'll be representing both you and the seller. Nothing for you to worry about.

AGENT RIGHT: Folks, you want your agent or broker to represent you and only you. Looking out for your needs and getting you the best deal should be your agent's top priorities.

BUYER: What if I decide to work with you and I don't think things are working out the way they should?

AGENT: Just let me know what you want me to do, and I'll do it.

AGENT RIGHT: You should have two or three options here. One, explain what is not working and explain how it should work. Two, explain it one last time. Three, terminate the agreement and find someone else to work for you. You could skip number two. These options should be in writing.

BUYER: How does a real estate agent differ from a real estate broker?

AGENT: A real estate agent works for a real estate broker, whereas a broker may actually own the real estate company. Otherwise, they pretty much provide the same services.

AGENT RIGHT: I would also add that a broker's license requires additional education and related experience and that it's the designated broker or broker-in-charge who is ultimately accountable for all company operations, policies, and procedures. Whether you choose to hire an agent or a broker, all of the questions and answers in this book apply.

BUYER: What's a buyer's broker, and do I need one?

AGENT: A buyer's broker works for the buyer only but may charge the buyer a fee. There's no real advantage to having one.

AGENT RIGHT: A buyer's agent or buyer's broker is definitely worth considering as they are legally obligated to represent the buyer and the buyer only. Furthermore, since their experience is primarily in assisting buyers, they may be

- better at finding the homes that best meet your specific requirements, and
- better at negotiating price and terms that are most advantageous to you.

BUYER: Can you help me get a mortgage?

AGENT: Yes, I know some very good mortgage companies and loan officers who can help you.

AGENT RIGHT: Good agents only use good loan officers. The right agents probably got rid of the wrong loan officers in the beginning of their real estate careers. So when you hire the right agent, you are sure to be referred to the right lender and loan officer as well. That would be the loan officer with the best rates, terms, and flexibility to work hand in hand with you and your agent to get you the best overall real estate deal.

BUYER: How many homes should I see before buying one?

AGENT: After a day or two of looking, you'll know which one you want to buy.

AGENT RIGHT: Looking at homes can be and should be fun but can also be exasperating. It's best to have a realistic idea of the home you'd like to buy. Make a list of the features that you must have and those that you would like to have. Give that list to your agent. Think about features that help or hurt resale value. That's important also. Search online to see what's available. Ask your agent to give you the best link for searching and comparing properties. Your agent should be searching as well. Have your agent show you the houses that best meet your criteria. Keep track of the properties you see. Rate the houses that you see. Discard the ones that won't work. That's one way to zero in on your dream house.

BUYER: How can I find out more about FSBO homes that are available for sale?

AGENT: I don't have a list of them. They're advertised in the newspaper. But you'll have a better chance of finding what you want by looking at homes that are currently listed.

AGENT RIGHT: That may be true. But you don't want to rule out FSBOs (homes that are for sale by owner), especially if there's one out there that's perfect for you. And they're not only advertised in the newspapers. You can also find them in For Sale by Owner magazines and For Sale by Owner online services. If you see one that you like, work with your agent to look at it and compare it to the other homes that you're interested in. Even though a FSBO may not be listed on the MLS (multiple listing service), the right agent can be extremely helpful in determining its value and in purchasing the FSBO as well. Incidentally, most homeowners who are selling their homes on their own are willing to pay some commission to the agent who brings in a buyer.

BUYER: Is it better to buy a new home or an older home?

AGENT: Working with a builder on a new home can be a headache. You'll probably get a better deal on a resale home.

AGENT RIGHT: There's no right answer in deciding whether to build new or buy existing. It really depends on what you want and current market conditions. Either way can be a good deal. You might even get a better deal on a new home. For example, some builders offer incredible financing packages that are only available when buying a new home. So don't rule out any of your options. Work with your agent, and decide what you want and what works best for you.

BUYER: How do I determine the value of the home that I am interested in buying?

AGENT: Look at homes with similar features and amenities and compare their prices to the home you want to buy. That will give you a good idea of the value of the home you are interested in.

AGENT RIGHT: That's a good start. As you look at different homes, you will begin to get an idea of comparative value. But the determination of the market value of a home is based upon many different factors. These factors include, but are not limited to, number of bedrooms, number of baths, finished square footage, total square footage, size of the garage, condition of the home, quality of the mechanicals, size of the lot, location of the home, and more. But you know something? Smart buyers won't buy overpriced homes, and the right agents won't let them. So while you're looking and comparing, let Agent Right prepare a comparative market analysis. That analysis will help you determine the value of the home in the same way that it helped the seller price the home. As an added benefit, it can also be utilized when you decide to make an offer.

BUYER: I've found my dream home. Now what?

AGENT: Let's make an offer and buy it.

AGENT RIGHT: I agree. But let's first look at the next chapter on purchase agreements.

Purchase Agreements

You get a call from your agent that an offer has been written on your home. They want to present it this evening. You're excited. You're also anxious. You hope it's a good offer. After all, your home is special, and you want to get as much as you can.

Or you've found the perfect house and you're ready to make an offer. You want to pay less than the seller is asking. You need to include certain conditions as well. But you don't want to insult the seller by offering too little. Especially since this is the perfect house. Maybe it's worth every penny of what the sellers are asking. How do you know how much to offer? How do you present the offer without offending the seller?

Welcome to the purchase agreement: how to write it, how to read it, how to negotiate it, and how to get the best deal.

Here are the questions and answers that relate to purchase agreements:

BUYER: What exactly is a purchase agreement?

AGENT: It's the written offer that you make for the home.

AGENT RIGHT: It's more than that. It's *the* written document that dictates how the rest of the sale will be handled. Sometimes called the "sales offer," it includes how much will be paid, when it will be paid, how it will be paid, and when the buyers take possession. It also includes buyer contingencies, seller disclosures, home warranties, repairs agreed to by the seller, and the length of time the seller has to respond to the offer.

When you are ready to make your offer, tell your agent. Your agent will be more than ready to write it up. Take your time and be sure to include all of your conditions and contingencies. If you want the seller to do something or pay for some repairs, it has to be written into the purchase agreement.

BUYER: If it is a new home, can I negotiate the price?

AGENT: Not really. For new homes, the base price of the house and the prices for special features and upgrades are fixed amounts. All you can do is add or delete what features and upgrades you want.

AGENT RIGHT: That's not totally true. Just as you can negotiate on a resale home, you can negotiate on a new home. This may come as a big surprise to many buyers, but the right agent will assist you in obtaining valuable buyer incentives, features, or upgrades at no cost to you.

BUYER: I've heard that it's a good idea to offer about 10 percent less than the asking price. Is this true?

AGENT: If you go in with a low bid, you may insult the seller and lose the home. Better go in with your best price.

AGENT RIGHT: Folks, here's how it really works. Different houses and different market conditions require different strategies. For example, in a seller's market, the seller may not come down on the price at all. You may see multiple offers. You may even see bidding wars between multiple buyers. And yes, you may lose that house.

On the other hand, in a buyer's market, you may find sellers coming down more than 10 percent on their price. You may also see sellers offering some very attractive terms, not to mention buyer incentives from agents and brokers as well. Buyer incentives from agents and brokers may include the following:

- free home warranty
- free home inspection
- decorating allowance
- moving allowance
- cash rebate

And finally, some houses may be so overpriced that even if you pay 10 percent less, you'd still be paying too much. It's very important to have an excellent understanding of house values and the housing market as well. That's why I recommend that you use your judgment and the expertise and advice of your Agent Right when deciding how much to offer.

BUYER: What are contingencies, and how do they work?

AGENT: They are conditions that you may want to include when buying your home.

AGENT RIGHT: Contingencies are conditions that you may include in the purchase agreement when you offer to buy a home. The seller is asked to agree to these conditions before you agree to buy the home. The seller may accept, reject, or negotiate these conditions with the buyer. All contingencies must be agreed upon before the purchase agreement is considered to be accepted.

BUYER: Are there any contingencies that I should include when making the offer?

AGENT: How much you want to pay, when you want to close, when you want to move in, and maybe a home inspection.

AGENT RIGHT: Here are some other contingencies (conditions that protect you) that you may want to consider:

- existing home sale
- loan preapproval

- commitment approval
- termite inspection
- time of sale inspection
- possession date
- assessment proration
- personal property included
- association regulations review
- financial statements review
- closing costs proration
- final walk-through

The home buyer will pay for the inspection as the inspector is working for them. Make sure it's a complete home inspection—and it's always good to be present during the entire inspection.

BUYER: How many of these contingencies should I include?

AGENT: The fewer contingencies, the better chance you'll have of getting the house for the price you want to pay.

AGENT RIGHT: Not necessarily. I've seen situations where the buyer had a lot of contingencies and the seller accepted the buyer's price when some of them were removed. So the contingencies were used like bargaining chips. Bottom line is be reasonable, but at the same time, protect yourself against unnecessary problems and expenses. It also depends on the current market. If it's a seller's market, they'll probably go with the offer that has fewer contingencies. Another factor to consider is the condition of the home. If repairs are needed, see what you can do yourself and what you can't do. Finally, compare the value of the home to other homes that are either for sale or have just been sold. If the home is a great deal as is, then just include the must-have conditions. Otherwise, include all the contingencies that will make this purchase a very good deal for you.

BUYER: What happens after the seller receives my offer?

AGENT: The seller will review it with his or her agent, and the agent will let us know if it is accepted, rejected, or if there are any counteroffers.

AGENT RIGHT: That's about what happens, but having the right agent can make a difference in making or breaking the deal. For example, it's important that your agent present the offer in person and state the terms clearly and tactfully. It's also a good idea to convey to the seller the buyer's rationale (e.g., price, terms, and contingencies) where appropriate. Selling a home is a business transaction, but it's also an emotional experience. Some agents take the time to tell the sellers about the buyers and explain why their home is perfect for them. Some bring pictures of the buyers to make the buy-sell process more personal. After your agent presents the offer, he or she will be asked to wait outside while the sellers and their agent review the offer.

BUYER: How much earnest money should I put down?

AGENT: About a $1,000, maybe $2,000. That should be enough.

AGENT RIGHT: It depends on the price of the house, the current market conditions, and the geographic location, and it's usually between 1 and 5 percent of the offered price. The bottom line is to demonstrate good faith and show how serious you are about buying the home. I have seen many buyers put down a substantial amount of earnest money, which made their offer more attractive and more likely to be accepted by the seller. That's a very good negotiating strategy for buyers. When sellers see more earnest money, they equate that to a more secure and better deal.

BUYER: Should I do an inspection before buying this home?

AGENT: It looks like new. I'm sure they took care of this home. But it's your choice.

AGENT RIGHT: Even if it looks like a new home, it is a good idea to have an inspection. When compared to the cost of the home, an inspection is a small price to pay for the assurance of knowing that there is nothing mechanically or structurally wrong with the home. If the inspector finds any problems, big or small, the costs of correcting them (which then become the seller's responsibility or are negotiated between the buyer and the seller) will usually amount to much more than the cost of the inspection.

BUYER: How much does an inspection cost, and how long does it take to do?

AGENT: An inspection will cost about $300, and it takes an hour to complete.

AGENT RIGHT: An inspection will cost somewhere between $300 and $600, and it will take one to four hours to complete. The cost and time is based upon the type of home, the age of the home, the size of the home, and the number and type of mechanical systems in the home.

BUYER: What does the inspector usually look at when doing an inspection?

AGENT: The inspector usually does a complete home inspection and looks at everything, so you are assured that the house is safe to live in and that it is a good value.

AGENT RIGHT: No, that's not right. A safe place to live with no structural or mechanical problems? Yes. Everything is in good condition and working properly? Yes. A good value for the money? No. The inspector will check the following:

- plumbing
- electrical connections
- heating, ventilation, and air-conditioning
- foundation/walls/attic for moisture and mold
- water heater
- waste disposal
- appliances
- doors, windows, floors, and ceilings
- roof and chimney
- siding
- land terrain and sloping
- possible presence of pests

In addition to checking for problems, an inspector can also give you an idea of estimated cost for repairs that may be needed.

It's important to know that if the home inspector finds any serious potential problems, he or she may suggest that an inspector with specialized expertise be hired to make the determination. For example, a potential problem with the furnace or air conditioner might call for certification by a licensed HVAC inspector. Or the presence of what appears to be mold in the attic or the basement might call for a review by a licensed engineering company that is certified in mold detection and eradication. In these instances, the buyer would usually request that the seller obtain the required certifications and make repairs if required. If the seller will not agree to obtain the certifications or make the repairs, the buyer may cancel the purchase agreement and get back the earnest money. Or if the buyer feels that the house defects are too serious, the buyer may cancel the purchase agreement as well.

SELLER: Now that an offer is coming in, what should we do before the purchase agreement is presented to us?

AGENT: Nothing. We'll wait to see what it is; then we'll make a decision.

AGENT RIGHT: Doing nothing is not the best choice. Now's the perfect time to be better prepared. We can review the initial CMA and see if the suggested price range needs to be adjusted. Better yet, we can update the initial CMA to factor in current active listings, current sold listings, and current market conditions. This would be very useful in gauging the offer and considering counteroffer strategies as well.

SELLER: What exactly is earnest money?

AGENT: It's the monetary deposit that the buyers include with their purchase agreement.

AGENT RIGHT: It is money that the buyers put down to show that they are serious about buying the house. Although it's stipulated in the purchase agreement, it's not given to the listing broker until the purchase agreement is accepted. It's usually a personal check that is made payable to the listing company and deposited in the listing broker's escrow account. If the buyer backs out of the deal for reasons that are not covered in the purchase agreement, the buyer may have to forfeit the earnest money. Sellers do have the option to request that the earnest money be forfeited if the buyer backs out for any reason.

SELLER: What happens if we can't reach an agreement?

AGENT: We'll keep countering. I'm sure we'll work it out.

AGENT RIGHT: (I want you to remember that phrase "I'm sure we'll work it out.") If we are getting closer, but not there yet, we can include a brief letter with our best and final offer and our reasoning for the offer. Sometimes, this personal approach will do the trick. Here's something else that happens once in a blue moon (or more frequently when everyone is trying to work it out): the agents offer to split the difference and give up some of their commission if the buyer and seller will come to an agreement. Now that would be a win-win resolution for everybody!

Addendums and Amendments

Okay, so you have a pretty good idea of what this purchase agreement is all about. But there are also various forms that may have to be included with the purchase agreement. These forms are called addendums and amendments.

I remember sitting in a real estate class many years ago when I was a real estate rookie. Someone asked the instructor why there were so many forms, and his answer was "Job security. The more forms, the more complex the transaction, and the more they need you." The class had a good laugh. But the state's real estate commission and the local municipalities weren't laughing. They enacted laws and developed forms that would protect the consumer when buying or selling real estate. The local realtor associations weren't laughing either. They standardized the purchase agreement. They also published forms that added consistency, reduced ambiguity, and lessened liability for their members when preparing real estate contracts.

From state to state, there are typically several forms that the real estate commission, the municipalities, and the local realtor associations require or recommend their members to use. That doesn't mean that you have to use all of them. But the right agent will use the right forms to protect your interests and to get you the best deal.

Here are the questions and answers that relate to addendums and amendments:

BUYER/SELLER: So which forms do we use to complete this real estate transaction?

AGENT: Just the standard purchase agreement and one or two miscellaneous addendums.

AGENT RIGHT: (Don't you wish it was that simple?) If you are a buyer, include an inspection addendum so that the purchase of the home is contingent on the inspection. You will also need a financing addendum—it is important because it specifies how you will pay for the home. Be sure to include a preapproval letter with the financing addendum. Do you have a home that you need to sell before you buy? If so, use a contingent upon sale of home addendum. That will make the purchase of your new home contingent upon the sale of your existing home so that you do not get stuck with two homes and two mortgages to pay.

If you are a seller, there is a real estate disclosure form that usually has to be completed. That form is used to confirm that everything in your home is in good working order and that you are unaware of any specific defects. Municipalities and lending institutions may require additional forms such as lead-base paint addendum, radon addendum, well disclosure, termite inspection, time-of-sale inspection, and building permits for major modification and remodeling projects.

BUYER/SELLER: What's the difference between addendums and amendments?

AGENT: They have different names, but they are both used for making additions or changes to the purchase agreement.

AGENT RIGHT: That's right. However, most addendums are usually preprinted and deal with conditions that have been standardized by local municipalities or realtor associations. On the other hand, amendments are usually blank forms that are used to negotiate other conditions not covered by existing addendums. For example, if the roof was very old, an amendment could be prepared to provide for a new roof.

BUYER: What is this real estate disclosure form that the seller included?

AGENT: It protects you by assuring you that everything in the house works or will be working before closing.

AGENT RIGHT: The scope of protection is much greater than that. In addition to disclosing what works or doesn't work, the real estate disclosure form requires that the seller disclose any known home defects such as cracked concrete, water intrusion, insect infestation, or anything else that they knew about while they were living there. This disclosure should be carefully reviewed before and during your home inspection.

BUYER: How can I use these addendums and amendments to further protect me?

AGENT: You can use these forms to request that repairs be made or that items be replaced.

AGENT RIGHT: In addition to requesting that repairs be made or that items be replaced, these forms will protect you by indicating which contractors will be used for doing these repairs or replacements. Some types of work (e.g., heating, air-conditioning, mold detection and eradication) should be completed by contractors who are certified to do that kind of work. Be sure to indicate who has agreed to pay for these repairs and that if the repairs that the seller agreed to make are not completed by closing, funds will be escrowed from the seller's proceeds. Addendums and amendments may also be used if the seller has agreed to pay for a home warranty or an appliance maintenance plan.

Finally, these purchase agreement-related forms may be used to describe any or all of the following conditions that the seller and buyer have agreed to:

- move-in agreements
- rent back agreements
- appliance or fixture exclusions
- personal property inclusions
- decorating allowances
- closing costs contributions

SELLER: Is there a special form to use to protect me if there's a problem with the buyer's financing down the road?

AGENT: Not really. Once we get the preapproval letter, that should do it.

AGENT RIGHT: Folks, that's the wrong answer. In addition to getting the preapproval letter, you also want to receive a full underwriting commitment no later than thirty days after the date of the finalized purchase agreement. That assures you that the buyer has been approved for this purchase in its entirety. Sometimes, a seller may require that the earnest money be forfeited if, for any reason, the buyer does not buy the house.

BUYER: How can these purchase agreement addendums and amendments get me the best deal?

AGENT: They can be used to your advantage when you negotiate price and terms.

AGENT RIGHT: That is correct. A skillful agent will know how and when to use these forms to your advantage when negotiating price and terms. For example, let's say the roof is seventeen years old. It doesn't leak, but it's getting close to its useful life expectancy (as indicated in the inspection report). This could be made a negotiable item. The buyer could ask the seller to replace the roof, provide a roof allowance, or lower the price of the house. The same rationale could be used for an old furnace, central air conditioner, or appliances.

BUYER: I'm planning to buy a home from a builder. Which forms should I use?

AGENT: The builder has all the forms that are needed to purchase the home. He or she can take care of it.

AGENT RIGHT: (Is the builder representing you? Absolutely not!) Even when you buy a home from the builder, you should still use the addendums and amendments that you and your agent feel are necessary to ensure that all of your concerns are fully satisfied. I strongly recommend using an agent to represent you in new construction. You will be pleasantly surprised by what the right agent can do for you when you're working with a builder. The right agent can obtain quality upgrades or additional amenities at no cost to you.

Closing the Deal

Yes! It's closing time! The deal is complete. The seller gets his money, the buyer gets her house, and everyone goes home happy. Nothing could go wrong. Right? Well, we sure hope so.

But a lot will be happening at the closing, and you have to be mentally alert and fully prepared for it. More importantly, your agent should have been preparing for it all along, making sure everything is in order, communicating with all the concerned parties, and coaching you along the way. And finally, your agent must be present at the closing to make sure that this last and critical step of the selling/buying process goes smoothly and is problem-free.

Here are the questions and answers that relate to closing the deal:

SELLER/BUYER: What exactly is a closing?

AGENT: That's when we all get together to finalize the transaction and transfer the title of the property.

AGENT RIGHT: Yep, that's the day everyone has been waiting for: the title is transferred and the sale becomes official. The closing is also when the real estate companies, title companies, or lawyers get paid. All closing costs will be listed in detail and charged to the seller and buyer. Throughout the real estate industry, specific types of closing costs are conventionally recognized as either seller costs or buyer costs, and they are charged accordingly. Alternatively, in the purchase agreement, the sellers and buyers may have already negotiated and agreed upon who will pay what closing costs.

SELLER/BUYER: What do you have to do for the closing?

AGENT: Nothing. We'll submit all the paperwork and then let the closers do their job.

AGENT RIGHT: The right real estate agent can do and will do much more. You need to have a mental picture of the closing process to understand what can be done to prevent problems. Depending upon what state you live in, the closing will be completed by title company employees, attorneys, paralegals, or real estate company staff. These closers do not have firsthand knowledge of your transaction. They may not be as familiar with all the paperwork submissions and specific details as your agent is. Therefore, it is extremely important that your real estate agent submit a closing information sheet along with the purchase agreement, loan approval, and other paperwork. The information sheet is sent to the closers, the mortgage company, the seller, and the buyer. It contains contact and contract information, and it also highlights transaction items that may require special handling. It is this closing information sheet, in conjunction with your real estate agent's proactive follow-up, that will keep the transaction and closing process on track!

SELLER: What is included in my closing costs?

AGENT: Mainly the commission and some other miscellaneous closing fees.

AGENT RIGHT: Don't ever accept an answer such as this! Ask for and get a seller's net sheet, which will list all of your closing costs given the selling price of the house and the terms of the purchase agreement. If you agreed to pay any of the buyer's closing costs, they will also be listed on the net sheet. It's also important to make sure that there are no liens on the house as they need to be paid or they will be deducted from net proceeds.

BUYER: What is included in my closing costs?

AGENT: Mainly the lender's fees and the closer's fees.

AGENT RIGHT: Don't accept an answer such as this either! You should have a good faith estimate from your mortgage lender. All of the known costs will be listed and described in the good faith estimate. If you agreed to any financial commitments for actions required by the mortgage company or local government, such as required repairs or property surveys, they will also be included in your closing costs. You will have to pay for a homeowner's insurance binder in order to close. This is also called hazard insurance, and it is required by the lender. Sometimes flood insurance for coastal properties is required, and that is usually an additional binder. It is important to note that although these costs will be paid at closing, the binders need to be in place before closing.

SELLER: Should I question any of these fees?

AGENT: The closers are pretty good, and the fees are usually accurate.

AGENT RIGHT: Yes, that may be true. But even so, you and your real estate professional still need to carefully review all of the closing costs that are charged to you. You would not believe how many mistakes are made!

BUYER: When will I know the exact closing costs?

AGENT: You'll get a HUD statement at closing with all the itemized costs.

AGENT RIGHT: Yes, you will get a HUD statement. HUD stands for Housing and Urban Development, a federal government agency. The HUD-1 statement is an itemized listing of the funds that are payable at closing. The totals at the bottom of the HUD-1 statement define the seller's net proceeds and the buyer's net payment at closing. The HUD-1 statement is also known as the "closing statement" or the "settlement sheet." It is prepared by the closers. And yes, you do get it at closing, but you and your agent may review it before closing as well. By the way, when you were prequalified by your mortgage lender, you should have received a good faith estimate of your closing costs. Now is the time to compare that sheet with your HUD-1. It should be almost identical. If it is not, your loan officer should be notified.

SELLER: Can closing costs be negotiated?

AGENT: They are set fees. Some are paid by the sellers, and others are paid by the buyers.

AGENT RIGHT: Yes, they are set fees. But as previously mentioned, closing costs may be negotiated in the purchase agreement. Are they customarily negotiated? No. Can they be negotiated? Of course.

BUYER: How can closing costs be reduced?

AGENT: They are already predetermined, fixed percentages costs that are computed based upon the sale price of the house.

AGENT RIGHT: The truth is that closing costs can be reduced or reallocated. Again, sellers and buyers may negotiate them in the purchase agreement. Once in a while, a mortgage company and loan officer will offer rebates for some of the closing costs. They do that because they want your business. And believe it or not, sometimes a real estate company, agent, or broker will pay for some of these costs.

SELLER: Who actually does the closing?

AGENT: The closers. There's one representing the seller and another representing the buyer.

AGENT RIGHT: That's right. And as previously stated, these closers may be title company employees, attorneys, paralegals, or real estate company staff. Though they conduct the closing, it is the real estate agent's responsibility to make sure the closers have the purchase agreement, the addendums, the amendments, and any other forms or instructions needed to get the job done.

BUYER: Is there anything that I need to do before the closing?

AGENT: Not a thing. The closing agent will take care of everything.

AGENT RIGHT: That's not correct. Now is the time to be proactive. Make sure that you receive and review a copy of the closing information sheet and all of the paperwork that your agent provided to the closer. If you find any mistakes or you believe that some information has not been provided, let your agent know. Then follow up with your agent to make sure that the closers have the corrected information. Call the closer, introduce yourself, and ask if they need anything else.

BUYER: What if some contingencies in the purchase agreement haven't been met?

AGENT: Oh, we'll work them out at the closing.

AGENT RIGHT: You don't ever want to be in that position. The closing is not the time to "work them out." Have your agent or your closer, or both of them, get everything in order before the closing. For example, if the inspection contingency form required that a repair be made and paid for by the seller and the repair cannot be completed until after closing, make sure that the cost of the repair is deducted from the seller's net proceeds and put in escrow (usually they deduct one and a half times the written estimate for the repair).

SELLER: Is there anything I need to bring to the closing?

AGENT: You'll get a letter from the closer.

AGENT RIGHT: Yes, you will get a letter. But it's safe to say that you'll need a driver's license or state-issued picture ID, your social security number, and maybe even a list of where you have lived for the past ten years.

BUYER: What do I have to bring to the closing?

AGENT: The closer will let you know.

AGENT RIGHT: You will need your driver's license or state-issued picture ID and your social security number. Sometimes, you will be asked where you lived for the past ten years. You will also need a bank check for funds due and an insurance binder if not previously provided.

SELLER: When do I have to vacate my house?

AGENT: Right after the closing.

AGENT RIGHT: Maybe yes, maybe no. There may be a separate addendum or amendment that addresses when the house is to be vacated. If not, then you vacate according to the date and time specified in the purchase agreement.

BUYER: When do I get possession of my house?

AGENT: Right after the closing.

AGENT RIGHT: Once again, we have to check the purchase agreement to see what possession date and time was agreed upon.

BUYER: I bought this house from you last winter. Now it's summer, it's hot as heck, and the darn air-conditioning isn't working. What do we do?

AGENT: Hold on. Who are you? Do I know you?

SECRETARY: Oh, he no longer works here.

RECORDING: You have reached a nonworking number or a number that has been disconnected. Blah, blah.

AGENT RIGHT: Hey, Stoller, like that's not even funny. Come on now, you have to help me out here. I mean, you know, these folks bought your book. They paid good money. You can't leave them hanging like that.

LARRY STOLLER: Okay, so the air-conditioning isn't working. It's hot as heck. But you'll still be cool. That's because your agent bought you a one-year homeowner warranty that covers all mechanicals and appliances. It was your closing gift when you purchased the house. That's right. I'm talking about Agent Right!

Some Additional Advice

If you decide to use an agent, and I suggest that you do, in some kind of capacity, think one, two, three!

ONE. Decide what role you want to play and what work you want to do. Decide what work you want the agent or broker to do.

TWO. Interview at least three agents from different companies, ask them the right questions, and get the right answers. Share the above information with the agents you are interviewing, and ask them how they can help you realize your specific goals and save you time and money while doing so.

THREE. Rate the agents by the questions you ask them, the answers they give you, and the information from Agent Right. Consider your comfort level with each agent, and choose the agent who will work best for you.

Now, folks, can I cover everything that could happen in this book? No. I cannot. But my intent was to hit the hot items and significant stuff. So if you have any questions or answers that you'd like to discuss, please e-mail me at LarryStoller@FindingAgentRight.com.

If you would like to get a head start in finding your Agent Right in your geographic area, please consult my web site at FindingAgentRight.com. There you will find a list of real estate agents who will tell you why they believe that they are the right agents for you.

Glossary

addendum. A blank form or a preprinted form to cover a specific condition, used to make an addition or change to a real estate contract.

agreement. Contractual arrangement in real estate that must be in writing in order to be binding.

affordability analysis. A detailed analysis of your ability to afford the purchase of a home. An affordability analysis takes into consideration your income, liabilities, and available funds, along with the type of mortgage you plan to use, the cost of living in the geographic area where you want to purchase a home, and the closing costs that you might expect to pay.

agent. A person licensed to negotiate the sale and/or purchase of real estate on behalf of a property owner or prospective buyer. An agent's license is held by the designated broker or broker-in-charge of the real estate company.

Agent Right. That specific real estate agent or broker who will best satisfy all of your selling *and*/or buying needs while providing you the level of professional competence and personal comfort that you require. "And" is in italics because if you are both selling and buying and entrusting both transactions to one individual, make sure you receive something extra and special for that!

amendment. A blank form used to make an addition or change to a real estate contract.

amenity. A feature of real estate that enhances its attractiveness and increases the occupant's satisfaction though the feature is not essential to the property's use. Natural amenities include a desirable location near

51

water and/or scenic views of the surrounding area. Human-made amenities include swimming pools, tennis courts, community buildings, and other recreational facilities.

application. A form used to apply for a mortgage loan and to record pertinent information concerning a prospective mortgagor.

appraisal. A written analysis of the estimated market value of a property prepared by a qualified appraiser; lender prerequisite before final approval of a home loan.

appraised value. An opinion of a property's fair market value based on an appraiser's analysis of the property, market, knowledge, and experience.

appraiser. A person who is licensed and qualified by education, training, and experience to estimate the value of real property and personal property.

appreciation. An increase in the value of a property due to changes in market conditions or other causes. The opposite of depreciation.

assessed value. The valuation placed on property by a public tax assessor for purposes of taxation.

attorney-in-fact. One who holds a power of attorney from another to execute documents on behalf of that person.

betterment. An improvement that increases property value as distinguished from repairs or replacements that simply maintain value.

bill of sale. A written document that transfers title to personal property.

binder. A preliminary agreement, secured by the payment of an earnest money deposit, under which a buyer offers to purchase real estate.

bridge loan. A form of short-term loan that is collateralized by the borrower's present home that is for sale. It allows the proceeds to be used for closing on a new house before the present home is sold. Also known as "swing loan."

broker. In real estate, a person who, for a commission or fee, brings parties together and assists in negotiating contracts between them. A broker's license is required in order to start a real estate company. An agent or a broker may be licensed under a broker-owner and conduct real estate business. The education and experience requirements for a broker are greater than what is required for an agent.

brokerage. A real estate company engaged in the act of bringing together two or more parties in exchange for a fee or a commission.

buyer incentive. Something of value offered to the buyer from the brokerage when the buyer purchases a property through that company.

buyer's broker. A real estate broker who exclusively represents the buyer's interests in a transaction.

buyer's market. A slow real estate market with more homes available and less buyers in which the buyers have the advantage.

cancellation clause. A clause that details the conditions under which each party, buyer or seller, may terminate the agreement.

CMA. An often used-acronym for a comparative market analysis. The CMA is a detailed written analysis of how much a specific property should sell for and how that property should be marketed.

certificate of title. A statement provided by a title company or attorney stating that the title to real estate is legally held by the current owner.

clear title. A title that is free of liens or legal questions as to ownership of the property.

closing. A meeting at which a sale of a property is finalized by the buyer signing the mortgage documents and paying closing costs and the seller signing the transfer documents and paying closing costs. Also called "settlement."

closer's fee. A fee or amount that a home buyer or home seller must pay at closing to a title company or an attorney for conducting the closing.

closing fee. A fee or amount that a home buyer or home seller must pay at closing to a title company or an attorney that is directly related to the closing function. These fees will be included as numbered items on the HUD-1 statement.

closing costs. Expenses over and above the price of the property incurred by buyers and sellers that are paid at closing to title companies, attorneys, lenders, insurance companies, and other vendors when transferring ownership of a property. Closing costs normally include origination fees, additional mortgage-related costs, prorated property taxes, transfer of deed taxes, amounts placed in escrow, charges for obtaining title insurance and/or required surveys, closer's fee, attorney's fee, and any other miscellaneous costs. Closing cost percentages may vary according to the area of the country. All of the closing costs are included as numbered items on the HUD-1 statement. Lenders and/or agents often provide estimates of closing costs to prospective home buyers and net proceeds estimates to home sellers.

closing statement. See HUD-1 statement.

cloud on title. Any conditions revealed by a title search that adversely affect the title to real estate. Clouds on title are usually removed by a quitclaim deed, release, or court action.

commission. The fee charged by a broker or agent for negotiating a real estate transaction. A commission is generally a percentage of the price of the property.

commitment letter. A formal offer by a lender stating the terms under which it agrees to lend money to a home buyer. It is also known as a "loan commitment."

comparables. An abbreviation for "comparable properties"; used for comparison in the appraisal process and the comparative market analysis. Comparables are properties similar to the property under consideration; they are those properties similar in size, location, and amenities that have recently been sold and/or are available for sale. Comparables help the appraiser or agent determine the approximate fair market value of the subject property.

condominium. A real estate project in which each unit owner has title to a unit in a building, an undivided interest in the common areas of the project, and sometimes the exclusive use of certain limited common areas.

contingency. A condition that must be met before a contract is legally binding. For example, home purchasers often include a contingency that specifies that the purchase agreement is not binding until the purchaser obtains a satisfactory home inspection report from a qualified home inspector.

contract. An oral or written agreement to do or not to do a certain thing: agreeing to terms and conditions in a purchase agreement for real estate. For real estate transactions, the contract must be in writing and signed by both parties to be legally binding.

cooperating broker. The broker in a multiple listing transaction from whose office a purchase agreement and negotiations leading up to a sale are originated.

counteroffer. A response to an offer that contains a different price or terms. In real estate, it must be in writing and signed by both parties to be binding.

credit. A reduction in the cost of a product or service.

deed. The legal document conveying title to a property.

disclosure. A statement to a potential buyer listing information relevant to a piece of property, such as the presence of any known defects.

discount points. One-time charges by the lender for originating a loan. A point is 1 percent of the amount of the mortgage.

down payment. The part of the purchase price of a property that the buyer pays in cash and does not finance with a mortgage.

dual agency. A relationship in which the real estate agent or broker represents both parties in a transaction.

earnest money deposit. A deposit made by the potential home buyer to show that he or she is serious about buying the house.

encroachment. An improvement that intrudes illegally on another's property.

encumbrance. Anything that affects or limits the title to a property, such as mortgages, leases, liens, or other restrictions.

equity. The difference between the market value of a house and the amount that is owed on the house.

escrow. An item of value, usually money, deposited with a third party to be delivered upon the fulfillment of a condition. For example, the deposit of earnest money with a real estate company when making an offer to purchase a home or funds deposited with an attorney or title company that will be disbursed at the closing of a real estate transaction.

escrow account. The account in which a real estate company holds the deposit of earnest money or where a mortgage servicer holds the borrower's escrow payments prior to paying property expenses.

examination of title. The report on the title of a property from the public records that confirms ownership of the property and that identifies encroachments and encumbrances on the property.

exclusive buyer's agreement. A written contract that gives the real estate agent or broker the exclusive right to represent the buyer in a transaction and details how and by whom the fee or commission is to be paid.

exclusive listing agreement. A written contract that gives a real estate agent or broker the exclusive right to sell a property for a specified time. It also specifies the amount of compensation that the seller will pay at closing.

fair market value. The price range that is defined by the highest price that a buyer will pay for a property and the lowest price that a seller would accept.

feedback. Information given to the seller related to property previews and showings.

final approval. A written commitment by the lender indicating that all conditions have been met and that the buyer is approved for the loan on the home that is being purchased as indicated in the purchase agreement and respective addendums and/or amendments.

firm commitment. A lender's written agreement to make a loan to a specific borrower on a specific property (usually required by a seller from a buyer as a purchase agreement contingency).

fishy agent. Has good taste, doesn't taste good, and doesn't give you the answers you're looking for. It's probably Agent Wrong.

fixture. Personal property that becomes real property when attached in a permanent manner to real estate.

flood insurance. Insurance that compensates for physical property damage resulting from flooding. It is required for properties located in federally designated flood areas.

FSBO. A home that is for sale by the owner. It is usually not on the multiple listing service (MLS), though some may be. The right real estate agent can be extremely valuable in assisting in the purchase of a FSBO.

401(k)/403(b). An employer-sponsored investment plan that allows individuals to set aside tax-deferred income for retirement or emergency purposes *and may allow loans for limited real estate purposes*. 401(k) plans are provided by employers that are private corporations. 403(b) plans are provided by employers that are nonprofit organizations.

401(k)/403(b) loan. Some administrators of 401(k)/403(b) plans allow for loans against the monies accumulated in these plans. Monies must be repaid to avoid serious penalty charges. Loans for limited real estate purposes may waive penalty charges.

good faith estimate. A written estimate of what your closing costs will be that is given to you by your loan officer when you begin the loan application process.

grantee. The person to whom an interest in real property is conveyed.

grantor. The person conveying an interest in real property.

hazard insurance. Insurance coverage that compensates for physical damage to a property from fire, wind, vandalism, or other hazards.

home inspection. A thorough visual inspection that evaluates the structural and mechanical condition of a property. A satisfactory home inspection is often included as a contingency by the purchaser.

home insurance. See **hazard insurance.**

homeowner's insurance. An insurance policy that combines personal liability insurance and hazard insurance coverage for a dwelling and its contents.

homeowner's warranty (HOW). A type of insurance that covers repairs to specified parts of a house for a given period of time. It can be provided by the builder or property seller as a condition of the sale.

HUD-1 statement. A required government document that is prepared at all closings, any time any property is sold. It is signed by the seller and buyer, and it includes an itemized listing of all of the funds that are payable at closing. Items that appear on the statement include real estate commissions, loan fees, discount points, and initial escrow amounts. Each item on the statement is represented by a separate number within a standardized numbering system. The total at the bottom of the HUD-1 statement define the seller's net proceeds and the buyer's net payment at closing. The blank form for the statement is published by the Department of Housing and Urban Development (HUD). The HUD-1 statement is also known as the "closing statement" or "settlement sheet."

income property. Real estate developed or improved to produce income.

inspection contingency. A type of contingency addendum that may be included in the purchase agreement. It adds a home inspection as a condition for buying or not buying the home if defects are identified that are not corrected and/or repaired as mutually agreed upon by seller and buyer.

insurance binder. A document that states that insurance is temporarily in effect. Because the coverage will expire by a specified date, a permanent policy must be obtained before the expiration date.

investment property. A property that is not occupied by the owner.

IRA (individual retirement account). A retirement account that allows individuals to make tax-deferred contributions to a personal retirement fund. Individuals can place IRA funds in bank accounts or in other forms of investment such as stocks, bonds, or mutual funds. Like 401(k) plans, IRAs may also allow loans for limited real estate purposes.

lease. A written agreement between the property owner and a tenant that stipulates the conditions under which the tenant may possess the real estate for a specified period of time and rent.

lender. A company or individual involved in making home loans. See mortgage banker; mortgage broker.

lien. A legal claim against a property that must be paid off when the property is sold.

listing. A piece of property placed on the market by a real estate agent.

listing agreement. A written contract that gives a licensed real estate agent the right to sell a property for a specified time and receive an agreed-upon payment.

listing price. The published price, in a listing service, at which a property is offered for sale by a real estate company and respective seller.

loan. A sum of borrowed money (principal) that is generally repaid with interest.

loan commitment. See **commitment letter**.

loan officer. A representative of a mortgage company, bank, or other financial or lending institution who solicits, initiates, and facilitates real estate loans.

loan origination. The process by which a mortgage lender brings into existence a mortgage secured by real property.

lock-in. A written agreement in which the lender guarantees a specified interest rate if a mortgage goes to closing within a set period of time. The lock-in also usually specifies the number of points to be paid at closing.

lock-in period. The time period during which the lender has guaranteed an interest rate to a borrower. See lock-in.

MLS (multiple listing service). A marketing organization of member brokers who agree to share their listings with one another. The listing information resides in a local, regional, or national database. This extensive repository of listings is also made available to the public in the hope of procuring more buyers for their properties more quickly than they could on their own.

market. A place where real estate can be bought and sold. It's also used to refer to the real estate economy during a certain period in time.

market condition. The state of the real estate economy during a certain period of time. It includes statistics such as number of sellers or buyers available, number of properties available, number of real estate transaction completed, time it takes to sell real estate, home appreciation rates, and current interest rates for mortgages.

market time. The time it takes for real estate to sell as calculated by the number of days the property has been on the market (i.e., the difference in the number of days from when the property was first available for sale until it was no longer available for sale).

market value. See **fair market value**.

mold. Fungus that may be present in a house, especially the type that could be harmful to the occupant's health (usually associated with water intrusion, water damage, or some other excess moisture condition).

mortgage. A legal document that pledges a property to a lender as security for payment of a debt. In the usual real estate transaction, the buyer seeks to borrow money to pay the seller the difference between the down payment and the purchase price of the property.

mortgage banker. A company that normally provides its own funds for mortgage financing and that originates mortgages exclusively for resale in the secondary mortgage market.

mortgage broker. An individual or company that brings borrowers and lenders together for the purpose of loan origination. Mortgage brokers typically require a fee or a commission for their services.

mortgagee. The lender in a mortgage agreement who receives and holds a mortgage as security for a debt.

mortgagor. The buyer/borrower in a mortgage agreement who is required to sign a promissory note for the amount borrowed and to execute a mortgage to secure the debt.

net proceeds estimate. A statement that details the amount of cash that the seller receives after paying all liens and closing costs associated with the sale of real estate property.

note. A legal document that obligates a borrower to repay a mortgage loan at a stated interest rate during a specified period of time.

offer. The promise and contract entered into by one party (the buyer) with another party (the seller) to purchase real estate property in exchange for an agreed-upon price and terms.

origination fee. A fee paid to a lender for processing a loan application. The origination fee is stated in the form of points. One point is 1 percent of the mortgage amount.

personal property. Any property that is not real property.

pest control. A procedure performed by a licensed contractor or individual to prevent and/or eradicate animal, bird, insect, and other infestations in a real estate property.

point. A one-time charge by the lender for originating a loan. A point is 1 percent of the amount of the mortgage.

power of attorney. A legal document that authorizes another person to act on one's behalf. A power of attorney can grant complete authority or can be limited to certain acts such as signing real estate contracts and closing documents.

property. See **real property**.

preapproval. The process in which a lender confirms that a perspective buyer has satisfied all of the lender's conditions for obtaining a loan for a real estate property listed at a specified price.

prequalification. The process in which a lender states that the financial condition of a perspective buyer has been reviewed and that it appears that he or she will be able to obtain a home loan up to a certain dollar amount.

property taxes. *Assessments* (monetary amounts) that are levied by a municipality on the value of all types of real property that must be paid by the owner of that property.

purchase agreement. A written contract (usually initiated by the buyer) signed by the buyer and seller stating the terms and conditions under which a property will be sold.

rate. The percentage of interest (i.e., 5 percent, 5 ½ percent, 5.75 percent, etc.) that a lender charges a borrower for a real estate loan for a specified period of time.

rate lock. A commitment issued by a lender to a borrower or other mortgage originator guaranteeing a specified interest rate for a specified period of time. See lock-in.

real estate. See real property. Real estate includes single-family homes, town homes, duplexes, condominiums, cooperatives, time shares, office buildings, apartment buildings, shopping centers, stores, land, and lots.

real estate agent. A person licensed to negotiate and transact the sale of real estate on behalf of the property owner.

real property. Land and appurtenances, including anything of a permanent nature such as structures, trees, minerals, and the interest, benefits, and inherent rights thereof.

realtors. A real estate broker or an associate who holds active membership in a local real estate board that is affiliated with the National Association of Realtors.

recorder. The public official who keeps records of transactions that affect real property in the area. Sometimes known as a "registrar of deeds" or "county clerk."

recording. The noting in the registrar's office of the details of a properly executed legal document, such as a deed, a mortgage note, a satisfaction of mortgage, or an extension of mortgage, thereby making it a part of the public record.

rent with option to buy. See **lease-purchase mortgage loan**.

sale-leaseback. A technique in which a seller deeds property to a buyer for a consideration and the buyer simultaneously leases the property back to the seller.

sales agreement. A written contract signed by the buyer and seller stating the terms and conditions under which a property will be sold.

seller's market. A fast real estate market with less available properties and more buyers in which the sellers have the advantage.

selling price. The listing price for a real estate property.

settlement. See **closing**.

settlement sheet. See **HUD-1 statement**.

time-of-sale inspection. A home inspection that is required by a local municipality before the home can be sold.

title. A legal document evidencing a person's right to or ownership of a property.

title company. A company that specializes in examining and insuring titles to real estate.

title insurance. Insurance that protects the lender (lender's policy) or the buyer (owner's policy) against loss arising from disputes over ownership of a property.

title search. A check of the title records to ensure that the seller is the legal owner of the property and that there are no liens or other claims outstanding.

transaction. The sale and/or purchase of real estate in its entirety, including the offer, counteroffers, acceptance, and the closing.

transfer of title. Any means by which the ownership of a property changes hands. Lenders consider all of the following situations to be a transfer of ownership: the purchase of a property "subject to" the mortgage, the assumption of the mortgage debt by the property purchaser, and any exchange of possession of the property under a land sales contract or any other land trust device. In cases in which an inter vivos or revocable trust is the borrower, lenders also consider any transfer of a beneficial interest in the trust to be a transfer of ownership.

transfer tax. State or local tax payable when title passes from one owner to another.